THE COM
RUNNER'S
DAY-BY-DAY LOG
2016 CALENDAR

Andrews McMeel
Publishing, LLC
Kansas City • Sydney • London

MARTY JEROME

2015

January

S	M	T	W	T	F	S
				1	2	3
4	5	6	7	8	9	10
11	12	13	14	15	16	17
18	19	20	21	22	23	24
25	26	27	28	29	30	31

February

S	M	T	W	T	F	S
1	2	3	4	5	6	7
8	9	10	11	12	13	14
15	16	17	18	19	20	21
22	23	24	25	26	27	28

March

S	M	T	W	T	F	S
1	2	3	4	5	6	7
8	9	10	11	12	13	14
15	16	17	18	19	20	21
22	23	24	25	26	27	28
29	30	31				

April

S	M	T	W	T	F	S
			1	2	3	4
5	6	7	8	9	10	11
12	13	14	15	16	17	18
19	20	21	22	23	24	25
26	27	28	29	30		

May

S	M	T	W	T	F	S
					1	2
3	4	5	6	7	8	9
10	11	12	13	14	15	16
17	18	19	20	21	22	23
24	25	26	27	28	29	30
31						

June

S	M	T	W	T	F	S
	1	2	3	4	5	6
7	8	9	10	11	12	13
14	15	16	17	18	19	20
21	22	23	24	25	26	27
28	29	30				

July

S	M	T	W	T	F	S
			1	2	3	4
5	6	7	8	9	10	11
12	13	14	15	16	17	18
19	20	21	22	23	24	25
26	27	28	29	30	31	

August

S	M	T	W	T	F	S
						1
2	3	4	5	6	7	8
9	10	11	12	13	14	15
16	17	18	19	20	21	22
23	24	25	26	27	28	29
30	31					

September

S	M	T	W	T	F	S
		1	2	3	4	5
6	7	8	9	10	11	12
13	14	15	16	17	18	19
20	21	22	23	24	25	26
27	28	29	30			

October

S	M	T	W	T	F	S
				1	2	3
4	5	6	7	8	9	10
11	12	13	14	15	16	17
18	19	20	21	22	23	24
25	26	27	28	29	30	31

November

S	M	T	W	T	F	S
1	2	3	4	5	6	7
8	9	10	11	12	13	14
15	16	17	18	19	20	21
22	23	24	25	26	27	28
29	30					

December

S	M	T	W	T	F	S
		1	2	3	4	5
6	7	8	9	10	11	12
13	14	15	16	17	18	19
20	21	22	23	24	25	26
27	28	29	30	31		

2017

January

S	M	T	W	T	F	S
1	2	3	4	5	6	7
8	9	10	11	12	13	14
15	16	17	18	19	20	21
22	23	24	25	26	27	28
29	30	31				

February

S	M	T	W	T	F	S
			1	2	3	4
5	6	7	8	9	10	11
12	13	14	15	16	17	18
19	20	21	22	23	24	25
26	27	28				

March

S	M	T	W	T	F	S
			1	2	3	4
5	6	7	8	9	10	11
12	13	14	15	16	17	18
19	20	21	22	23	24	25
26	27	28	29	30	31	

April

S	M	T	W	T	F	S
						1
2	3	4	5	6	7	8
9	10	11	12	13	14	15
16	17	18	19	20	21	22
23	24	25	26	27	28	29
30						

May

S	M	T	W	T	F	S
	1	2	3	4	5	6
7	8	9	10	11	12	13
14	15	16	17	18	19	20
21	22	23	24	25	26	27
28	29	30	31			

June

S	M	T	W	T	F	S
				1	2	3
4	5	6	7	8	9	10
11	12	13	14	15	16	17
18	19	20	21	22	23	24
25	26	27	28	29	30	

July

S	M	T	W	T	F	S
						1
2	3	4	5	6	7	8
9	10	11	12	13	14	15
16	17	18	19	20	21	22
23	24	25	26	27	28	29
30	31					

August

S	M	T	W	T	F	S
		1	2	3	4	5
6	7	8	9	10	11	12
13	14	15	16	17	18	19
20	21	22	23	24	25	26
27	28	29	30	31		

September

S	M	T	W	T	F	S
					1	2
3	4	5	6	7	8	9
10	11	12	13	14	15	16
17	18	19	20	21	22	23
24	25	26	27	28	29	30

October

S	M	T	W	T	F	S
1	2	3	4	5	6	7
8	9	10	11	12	13	14
15	16	17	18	19	20	21
22	23	24	25	26	27	28
29	30	31				

November

S	M	T	W	T	F	S
			1	2	3	4
5	6	7	8	9	10	11
12	13	14	15	16	17	18
19	20	21	22	23	24	25
26	27	28	29	30		

December

S	M	T	W	T	F	S
					1	2
3	4	5	6	7	8	9
10	11	12	13	14	15	16
17	18	19	20	21	22	23
24	25	26	27	28	29	30
31						

2016

January

M	T	W	T	F	S
				1	2
4	5	6	7	8	9
11	12	13	14	15	16
18	19	20	21	22	23
25	26	27	28	29	30

February

S	M	T	W	T	F	S
	1	2	3	4	5	6
7	8	9	10	11	12	13
14	15	16	17	18	19	20
21	22	23	24	25	26	27
28	29					

March

S	M	T	W	T	F	S
		1	2	3	4	5
6	7	8	9	10	11	12
13	14	15	16	17	18	19
20	21	22	23	24	25	26
27	28	29	30	31		

April

M	T	W	T	F	S
				1	2
4	5	6	7	8	9
11	12	13	14	15	16
18	19	20	21	22	23
25	26	27	28	29	30

May

S	M	T	W	T	F	S
1	2	3	4	5	6	7
8	9	10	11	12	13	14
15	16	17	18	19	20	21
22	23	24	25	26	27	28
29	30	31				

June

S	M	T	W	T	F	S
			1	2	3	4
5	6	7	8	9	10	11
12	13	14	15	16	17	18
19	20	21	22	23	24	25
26	27	28	29	30		

July

M	T	W	T	F	S
				1	2
4	5	6	7	8	9
11	12	13	14	15	16
18	19	20	21	22	23
25	26	27	28	29	30

August

S	M	T	W	T	F	S
	1	2	3	4	5	6
7	8	9	10	11	12	13
14	15	16	17	18	19	20
21	22	23	24	25	26	27
28	29	30	31			

September

S	M	T	W	T	F	S
				1	2	3
4	5	6	7	8	9	10
11	12	13	14	15	16	17
18	19	20	21	22	23	24
25	26	27	28	29	30	

October

M	T	W	T	F	S
					1
3	4	5	6	7	8
10	11	12	13	14	15
17	18	19	20	21	22
24	25	26	27	28	29
31					

November

S	M	T	W	T	F	S
		1	2	3	4	5
6	7	8	9	10	11	12
13	14	15	16	17	18	19
20	21	22	23	24	25	26
27	28	29	30			

December

S	M	T	W	T	F	S
				1	2	3
4	5	6	7	8	9	10
11	12	13	14	15	16	17
18	19	20	21	22	23	24
25	26	27	28	29	30	31

INTRODUCTION

If not now, when? That may sound like an advertisement for a running shoe, but consider that it's the imperative by which we all live, whether we're starting a family or changing careers, paying the electric bill or exiting the freeway. Running makes us mindful of life's quotidian urgency.

You need only look at its stars. Alberto Salazar was the greatest distance runner in the world for most of the 1980s. You'd never have guessed it. Most elite distance runners are dancer-like in form—seeming to float, landing lightly, calves pulling heels to virtually graze their hams with each stride. Salazar was tall, gangly, and ungraceful. His coaches thought he was hopeless. So how did he come to win the New York City Marathon three consecutive times?

He shrugs it off to artless desire. Even as a boy, racing had brought him close to death on more than one occasion. In 2007, well after the apex of his career, Salazar collapsed on a practice field at the Nike campus where he was coaching, clinically dead for 14 minutes. In the moments that followed, rescuers administered CPR to feed oxygen to his brain and EMTs shocked his heart eight times with defibrillator paddles. Nine days later, he was back at the Nike campus demanding ever more from his runners. In his memoir, *14 Minutes*, he explains:

> "I had learned something from death. I had learned, through the agency of my lifelong prayer, that I wasn't afraid of death. I realized that this made me different from the people walking by me on the street. More important—at least to me in the midst of my obsession it made me different from other runners. I no longer doubted my toughness."

We have all dreamt of throwing everything we have into an important life event, whether it's a race or a solemn commitment to someone we love. But the moment and the magic rarely coincide. And sometimes you have to improvise. Boston Police superintendent Willia Evans crossed the finish line at tha fateful 2013 Marathon (3:34, aged 54). He had barely dropped into the whirlpool at the Boston Athleti Club afterward when news of the bombings surged through the cops who regularly soak there. Uniform lights and sirens to Berkeley Street at Columbus, Evans found himself staring at unimaginable horror—bodies, blood, blown-out windows. His personal aches from running a marathon only hours earlier were instantly dispatched.

What's often ignored in the mec is that the mop-up for public trage often takes weeks, even months. Fe Evans, the bombings at Boston we followed by a necessary presidentie visit. The police were trying to reassert public safety, but now the also had to deal with White House Secret Service. Evans's working hours ran long in the ensuing days. Up at 3:30 in the morning, he managed to squeeze a half-hour run into the dark morning before showing up for duty. He has since been promoted to Boston Police Commissioner.

Job promotions aside, what returns do you expect from training Consider how those who love you contribute to your workouts, then think about those who merely admire you. Running has the habit of blurring these distinctions. Cross-country coach Amy Farmer at Hinkley High School in Aurora, Colorado, manages a motley mess of runners. The kids are mostly poor, many illegal residents. Dozens of languages spill into the hallways between classes. Home life for these children is often dodgy, difficult for outsiders to understand in customs and expectations, and homes are rarely permanent. Parents are sometimes deported mid-semester. Teammates simply vanish. To those who make it to practice, Farmer has found that running is a fabric, a way of connecting one kid to the next, to American culture, however you view it.

She rarely produces track-and-field superstars, nor does she see the need. Yet the loyalty she captures is astonishing. Whether their native country is Mali, Mexico, or Eritrea, kids find a second family with Farmer and her husband, Chris Carhart, who coaches the track team. Both emphasize personal achievement over ribbons and trophies, even if it's just to get a team member across the finish line in any way possible. Training helps kids cope with the chaos of uprooted lives. The discipline and focus extend well beyond the workout at hand.

You already know how this works. Sure, running reaches into our lives in unexpected ways. Can it cure cancer? No athletic endeavor in the history of the world has tried harder to make it happen. Last year, American runners raised more than $650 million to fight the disease—

at thousands of events around the country. Curt Pesmen, a survivor of colon cancer at age 43, believes we need to consider it in new ways. "Yes, you can be cured of cancer. But that doesn't mean you'll ever truly leave it in your dust," he writes.

Eight weeks after surgery and chemo, the dedicated runner wanted to see if he could trot a familiar 1.5-mile loop near his home in North Boulder. He made it 10 steps. "I realized that even walking a *quarter* mile was out of the question." He needed a recovery training program—a series of post-cancer PRs. He set his long-term sights on the BolderBoulder, a 10K event. Along the way, he eschewed the cancer-survivor bandwagon that held up inspiration for so many runners. ("Nothing against the pink ribbons and all, but I wanted to hurt "normally," like a runner who absentmindedly forgets his glucosamine.")

The return journey was slow and often excruciating. Also, terribly lonely. When race day finally arrived, Pesmen surprised himself by shouting at the volunteers and the Gatorade table, "I'm a CANCER SURVIVOR!," punching the air with his fist: "If one day you find yourself running solo and screaming hugely, in an event a full decade after you got a life-threatening diagnosis and ended up weeping on the kitchen floor with your wife who just collapsed in your arms at the shock of it all . . . you've got to admit that cancer never really leaves your life all the way."

Nor, for that matter, does running.

—Marty Jerome ■

January

SUNDAY	MONDAY	TUESDAY	WEDNESDAY	THURSDAY	FRIDAY	SATURDAY
					1 New Year's Day Kwanzaa ends (USA)	2
3	4 New Year's Day (observed) (NZ) Bank Holiday (UK—Scotland)	5	6	7	8	9
10	11	12	13	14	15	16
17	18 Martin Luther King Jr.'s Birthday (observed) (USA)	19	20	21	22	23
24 31	25	26 Australia Day	27	28	29	30

"Bid me run, and I will striv
with things impossible.

—William Shakespear
Julius Caesa

FLESH

Drop your pants—right now. Shoo kids, pets, and other nosy intrusions. Find the biggest mirror you can, get naked, and behold. Simply stare at yourself, long and dispassionately. Don't judge; just evaluate, especially if you haven't indulged this exercise in years.

As you stare at the quite raw material from which your training program will proceed over the next 12 months, contemplate not how you want to change your body, but how your body should change your workouts.

Start with your head. Eyes should be clear of redness, puffiness, and that ineffable look of perpetual fatigue. If not, changes in your diet, in alcohol and caffeine consumption, or in the amount and quality of sleep you're getting should come under scrutiny. Chat with a high school track star the next time you can, about . . . anything. Chances are, clarity in the eyes, not a tight physique, will hold your attention. Yes, surging hormones, impossibly hard workouts, and the unjust gift of youth make bright eyes. But so does the fearlessness from unbroken ambitions and mortal insouciance—part body, part soul. When you stare into your own eyes, distinguish which from which. Let these inform your running goals for the coming year.

Now glance at your shoulders and arms. Check for proportion, just as a life-drawing class instructor would evaluate your sketches. When you have the legs of Ginger Rogers or Fred Astaire, but the arms of Don Knotts, your workouts are askew, and quite possibly so is your body's frame. Stronger upper-body muscle makes you a more efficient runner, less prone to injury from unbalanced loads. A little cross training won't kill you.

The upper abdomen is a regrettable American obsession, the measure by which too many runners judge their physical progress and moral virtue. If these are issues, promise that this year you will simply become a better runner, however you define it. Let your tummy tag along for the ride, and it will surely shrink, though not without abiding aid from every other corner of your life—diet, leisure activities, loved ones, and the vision you hold of what your body can become. As you nakedly stare into the mirror, see your future body as realistically as you can.

Do the same drill for your bum. Attempting to sculpt this part of the anatomy is a fool's errand for the vast majority of runners. Any regular training program will bring improvement. Better to invest your running ambitions in other areas, and be prepared for a pleasant surprise in what follows.

The great mysteries in the mirror are ankles and feet, which rarely expose trouble—while causing the meanest sorts. Obviously, persistent or recurrent swelling, bumps and lumps, obdurate or shifting pains, and stark discolorations should send you to the doctor. But so should many other small quirks. A runner's visual clues tell you only a little. Most medical opinions aren't much better. Even so, let all observers remind you that a stopwatch isn't the only way to evaluate yourself as a runner. ■

Distance carried forward: _____

28 Monday
_____
_____
_____

Where & When: _____ **Distance:** _____
Comments: _____
_____

29 Tuesday
_____
_____
_____

Where & When: _____ **Distance:** _____
Comments: _____
_____

30 Wednesday
_____
_____
_____

Where & When: _____ **Distance:** _____
Comments: _____
_____

31 Thursday
_____
_____
_____

Where & When: _____ **Distance:** _____
Comments: _____
_____

1 Friday
_____
_____
_____

Where & When: _____ **Distance:** _____
Comments: _____
_____

Dec 2015/Jan

Saturday 2

Where & When: Distance:

Comments:

Sunday 3

Where & When: Distance:

Comments:

© Tony Garcia/maXximages.com

tip: Don't wait for—instead, invent—the perfect opportunity to begin a training program.

Distance this week: Weight:

Distance carried forward:

4 Monday

Where & When: **Distance:**
Comments:

5 Tuesday

Where & When: **Distance:**
Comments:

6 Wednesday

Where & When: **Distance:**
Comments:

7 Thursday

Where & When: **Distance:**
Comments:

8 Friday

Where & When: **Distance:**
Comments:

January

Saturday 9

_____
_____
_____

Where & When: _____ **Distance:** _____
Comments: _____
_____

Sunday 10

_____
_____

Where & When: _____ **Distance:** _____
Comments: _____
_____

© Steve Glass/maXximages.com

tip: Exercise demonstrably lowers general anxiety in many people, perhaps because they perceive their environments as less threatening.

Distance this week: _____ **Weight:** _____

Distance carried forward:

11 Monday

Where & When: **Distance:**

Comments:

12 Tuesday

Where & When: **Distance:**

Comments:

13 Wednesday

Where & When: **Distance:**

Comments:

14 Thursday

Where & When: **Distance:**

Comments:

15 Friday

Where & When: **Distance:**

Comments:

Saturday 16

6

Where & When: _____   Distance: _____

Comments: _____

Sunday 17

7

Where & When: _____   Distance: _____

Comments: _____

tip: Lose the guilt. Men who run only once a week are still less likely to die prematurely than their couch-potato brethren.

Distance this week: _____   Weight: _____

Distance carried forward: _____

18 Monday

18

_____
_____
_____

Where & When: _____ **Distance:** _____
Comments: _____
_____

19 Tuesday

19

_____
_____
_____

Where & When: _____ **Distance:** _____
Comments: _____
_____

20 Wednesday

20

_____
_____
_____

Where & When: _____ **Distance:** _____
Comments: _____
_____

21 Thursday

2

_____
_____
_____

Where & When: _____ **Distance:** _____
Comments: _____
_____

22 Friday

22

_____
_____
_____

Where & When: _____ **Distance:** _____
Comments: _____
_____

January

Saturday 23

here & When: Distance:

mments:

Sunday 24

here & When: Distance:

mments:

© Bonninstudio/maXximages.com

ip: Baby your ankles. Hip and knee replacements are usually successful procedures these days. Ankle replacements are less so; they're more complicated with mixed results.

stance this week: Weight:

Distance carried forward:

25 Monday   2

Where & When: **Distance:**
Comments:

26 Tuesday   2

Where & When: **Distance:**
Comments:

27 Wednesday   2

Where & When: **Distance:**
Comments:

28 Thursday   2

Where & When: **Distance:**
Comments:

29 Friday   2

Where & When: **Distance:**
Comments:

January

Saturday 30

o

here & When: Distance:

omments:

Sunday 31

1

here & When: Distance:

omments:

"Opportunity follows struggle. It follows effort. It follows hard work. It doesn't come before."
—Shelby Steele

tip: Running not only makes your skin appear younger; it may also reverse skin aging in people who start exercising late in life.

otes:

istance this week: Weight:

February

SUNDAY	MONDAY	TUESDAY	WEDNESDAY	THURSDAY	FRIDAY	SATURDAY
	1	2	3	4	5	6 Waitangi Day (NZ)
7	8 Waitangi Day (observed) (NZ)	9	10 Ash Wednesday	11	12	13
14 St. Valentine's Day	15 Presidents' Day (USA)	16	17	18	19	20
21	22	23	24	25	26	27
28	29					

"Fail better."
—Samuel Beckett

SLAVE

If racing tosses you the occasional lesson in humiliation, training teaches humility, an enduring virtue. After all, you'll never master training. Succeed at a goal, and it's time to step up your game and work harder. Fail at a goal, and . . . well, work harder. Either way, you will always be servile to a routine.

So why do you stick with it? Too often, we see accomplishment only as a product of imperious will. Yet running empowers you in ways that can't be measured by numbers—miles, personal records, pounds shed, whatever. For example, most runners are healthier people than the sedentary lot, according to any manner of clocks and yardsticks. But the marathoner who limps away from the finish line only to be hit by a passing truck proves that none of us ever master our fates. Training teaches that, at best, you can make headway against the odds. What's more, it teaches that you have no other choice. Be humble about it.

Runners are more confident people, even when the evidence of their lives proves them fools. Intimately knowing your body's abilities and limitations informs many nonphysical things you do, whether it's your ability to size up a complex project at work or your capacity to love another person. Training teaches that you are always working with incomplete information. Relax. Trust and act on what you know. Everything else will sort itself out.

The psychological benefits go further. We've all read that a hard aerobic workout is as effective as antidepressants for reducing stress and anxiety. Why? Even the most over-trod running trail, as familiar as old boots, presents daily uncertainties—as it should—and no runner is a robot. You may crumple in agony from today's workout for no reason whatsoever. Training only shoved you out the door. Don't seek wisdom in the push. Just recognize that sometimes running into an abyss serves you long after you've showered and gone to bed. It doesn't dispel the uncertainties of life; it only makes the next big trouble easier to confront. Besides, it's cheaper than Prozac.

Smarter slaves let their masters speak for them, especially when problems are messy. Nothing clears the head of hectoring voices and dread like a hard run. Friends and loved ones may roll their eyes when you insist on a workout amidst some perceived crisis, even though these people benefit from the calmed mind that returns. Don't lecture on the matter—only another runner understands. Unless the calamity demands urgent attention (a sheriff pounding on the door, a flooded kitchen, a goodbye note from your suddenly vanished partner), excuse yourself and put on your running shorts. For an hour or so, leave all other matters to the sound of your feet striking the ground.

In fact, make all the people you care about accept that you are a slave to training. Strength is in the struggle. Don't bother to explain this. Just make sure everyone feels the crack of your whip. ■

Distance carried forward:

1 Monday
3

Where & When: Distance:
Comments:

2 Tuesday
3

Where & When: Distance:
Comments:

3 Wednesday
3

Where & When: Distance:
Comments:

4 Thursday
3

Where & When: Distance:
Comments:

5 Friday
3

Where & When: Distance:
Comments:

February

Saturday 6

Where & When: Distance:

Comments:

Sunday 7

Where & When: Distance:

Comments:

© Leo Himsl/maXximages.com

tip: Studies have proven time and again that bribing yourself won't keep you motivated. Nix the self-serving promises of dessert, a new wardrobe, or a longer lifespan. Learn to love training for itself.

Distance this week: Weight:

8 Monday   3

Where & When: **Distance:**

Comments:

9 Tuesday   4

Where & When: **Distance:**

Comments:

10 Wednesday   4

Where & When: **Distance:**

Comments:

11 Thursday   4

Where & When: **Distance:**

Comments:

12 Friday   4

Where & When: **Distance:**

Comments:

February

Saturday 13

4

_____

_____

_____

here & When: _____ Distance: _____

omments: _____

5

Sunday 14

_____

_____

_____

here & When: _____ Distance: _____

omments: _____

_____

tip: Set midway goals in your workouts. You're more likely to be pleased by the final results.

© Jose Luis Pelaez Inc./maXximages.com

istance this week: _____ Weight: _____

Distance carried forward:

15 Monday   4

Where & When: Distance:

Comments:

16 Tuesday   4

Where & When: Distance:

Comments:

17 Wednesday   4

Where & When: Distance:

Comments:

18 Thursday   4

Where & When: Distance:

Comments:

19 Friday   5

Where & When: Distance:

Comments:

February

Saturday 20

1

Where & When: Distance:
Comments:

2   **Sunday 21**

Where & When: Distance:
Comments:

© Joseph C. Dovala/maXximages.com

tip: Hill training doesn't require you to run directly to the stars. Where possible, mix steep climbs with long, gentle grades, up and down.

Distance this week: **Weight:**

Distance carried forward:

22 Monday   5

Where & When: Distance:
Comments:

23 Tuesday   5⁴

Where & When: Distance:
Comments:

24 Wednesday   5⁵

Where & When: Distance:
Comments:

25 Thursday   5⁶

Where & When: Distance:
Comments:

26 Friday   5⁷

Where & When: Distance:
Comments:

February

Saturday 27

8

_____

_____

_____

_____

here & When: _____ Distance: _____

omments: _____

_____

Sunday 28

9

_____

_____

_____

here & When: _____ Distance: _____

omments: _____

_____

"You may have to fight a battle more than once to win it."
—Margaret Thatcher

tip: Vitamin C and E supplements may actually hinder your training by making muscle cells less efficient at metabolizing glycogen.

otes: _____

_____

_____

_____

_____

istance this week: _____ Weight: _____

March

SUNDAY	MONDAY	TUESDAY	WEDNESDAY	THURSDAY	FRIDAY	SATURDAY
		1 St. David's Day (UK)	**2**	**3**	**4**	**5**
6 Mothering Sunday (Ireland, UK)	**7** Labour Day (Australia—WA)	**8** International Women's Day	**9**	**10**	**11**	**12**
13	**14** Eight Hours Day (Australia—TAS) Canberra Day (Australia—ACT) Labour Day (Australia—VIC) Commonwealth Day (Australia, Canada, NZ, UK)	**15**	**16**	**17** St. Patrick's Day	**18**	**19**
20 Palm Sunday	**21**	**22**	**23**	**24** Purim*	**25** Good Friday (Western)	**26** Easter Saturday (Australia—except TAS, W
27 Easter (Western)	**28** Easter Monday (Australia, Canada, Ireland, NZ, UK—except Scotland)	**29**	**30**	**31**		

*Begins at sundown the previous day

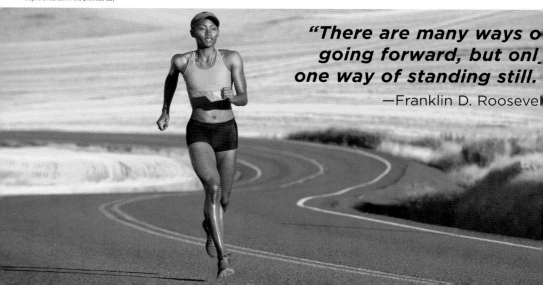

"There are many ways o going forward, but onl, one way of standing still.
—Franklin D. Roosevel

MURDER

Almost any failed training program enlists some measure of self-sabotage. Obviously, injury and illness can stop it cold with no one to blame, though killing it completely requires accomplices, principally you. So put yourself on trial before the crime is committed.

Even serious illness and injury eventually become history. Meanwhile, the psychological blow lingers long after physical miseries are subdued. It hurts to step back into a training routine, especially if you've been away for months. Progress will be slow. Your erstwhile abilities will taunt you all the way, discouragement everywhere you look. It's only reasonable to continue filling your customary training hours with Netflix. Yet this is exactly the point: Training should teach you that the love always returns, that the obstacles loom larger than their reality. Force yourself to commit to those initial workouts. Give yourself six dutiful, uninspiring weeks before you decide to quit. The smart money says you won't.

Dashed goals—a disastrous race performance, a cynical bathroom scale, whatever—let you slither away from the truth, but for how long? Rationalization is a coward's exit (*I'm not really cut out for this event; all this work and my butt still looks fat*). You may know your strengths as a runner, but are your ambitions realistic? Don't blame your feet for failure. The culprit is likely between your ears. Reevaluate your goals and get back to work. Consider it parole.

Outsized goals aren't the only ways to kill a training program, of course. Small frustrations often chip away at enthusiasm, especially when the first bursts of improvement plateau, giving way to the duller business of everyday workouts. There's no denying this essential tedium, and painting it up pretty only hastens discouragement. A change of routine and new goals are obvious remedies. But these only shift the moment. Pain and monotony are constants of running. Accept them. Use their familiar groove to learn to detach when necessary. They bank future rewards, first with a hot shower and the afterglow that comes with any workout, later with strength and endurance.

A lack of foresight will ice your ambitions as much as overreaching will. With only a little finesse, runners can accommodate most real-life interruptions—business travel, a pregnancy, a lengthy lawsuit—but a race date is nailed to the calendar. So is any other goal worthy of your effort. Obviously, we live in an endless river of contingencies. So let this fact inform your goals. Make hard plans early, then be flexible, daresay creative, in how you structure your workouts. Stay humble when the gravel gets kicked into the schedule.

When the training is calm and productive, put your goals in a lineup. Look for the criminals, especially the shifty kind that caught your imagination but then hung you out to dry. Take aim, fire. Training entails all manner of injustices, but you are forever the judge and jury. You are always free to go. ■

Distance carried forward: _____

29 Monday   6

_____
_____
_____

Where & When: _____   **Distance:** _____
Comments: _____
_____

1 Tuesday   6

_____
_____
_____

Where & When: _____   **Distance:** _____
Comments: _____
_____

2 Wednesday   6

_____
_____
_____

Where & When: _____   **Distance:** _____
Comments: _____
_____

3 Thursday   6

_____
_____
_____

Where & When: _____   **Distance:** _____
Comments: _____
_____

4 Friday   6

_____
_____
_____

Where & When: _____   **Distance:** _____
Comments: _____
_____

February/March

5

Where & When: Distance:

Comments:

6

Sunday 6

Where & When: Distance:

Comments:

© David Jakle/maXximages.com

tip: Strength-training exercises for hamstrings reduce running injuries. There's scientific evidence for this.

Distance this week: Weight:

Distance carried forward:

7 Monday   6

Where & When: Distance:
Comments:

8 Tuesday   6

Where & When: Distance:
Comments:

9 Wednesday   6

Where & When: Distance:
Comments:

10 Thursday   7

Where & When: Distance:
Comments:

11 Friday   7

Where & When: Distance:
Comments:

March

Saturday 12

2

here & When: Distance:

mments:

Sunday 13

3

here & When: Distance:

mments:

© Ty Milford/maXximages.com

tip: Pain and injury are different things, but the distinctions blur. When in doubt, stop your workout.

stance this week: Weight:

14 Monday

Where & When: **Distance:**

Comments:

15 Tuesday

Where & When: **Distance:**

Comments:

16 Wednesday

Where & When: **Distance:**

Comments:

17 Thursday

Where & When: **Distance:**

Comments:

18 Friday

Where & When: **Distance:**

Comments:

March

Saturday 19

here & When: _____ Distance: _____
omments: _____

Sunday 20

here & When: _____ Distance: _____
omments: _____

© Paul Bradbury/maXimages.com

tip: If you can't run because of injury, walk. Perhaps it's just common sense, but walking slows physical decline, making it easier to return to regular training once you've healed.

istance this week: _____ Weight: _____

Distance carried forward:

21 Monday   8

Where & When: Distance:

Comments:

22 Tuesday   8

Where & When: Distance:

Comments:

23 Wednesday   8

Where & When: Distance:

Comments:

24 Thursday   8

Where & When: Distance:

Comments:

25 Friday   8

Where & When: Distance:

Comments:

March

Saturday 26

here & When: Distance:

omments:

Sunday 27

here & When: Distance:

omments:

It's not always necessary to be strong,
but to feel strong."

—Jon Krakauer

tip: Running is no cure for attention-deficit hyperactivity disorder (ADHD), but it temporarily raises levels of dopamine, yielding results similar to the drugs Ritalin and Adderall.

otes:

istance this week: Weight:

April

SUNDAY	MONDAY	TUESDAY	WEDNESDAY	THURSDAY	FRIDAY	SATURDAY
					1	2
3	4	5	6	7	8	9
10	11	12	13	14	15	16
17	18	19	20	21	22 Earth Day	23 Passover* St. George's Day (UK)
24	25 Anzac Day (NZ, Australia)	26	27	28	29 Holy Friday (Orthodox)	30 Passover ends

*Begins at sundown the previous day

"Only those who dare
to fail greatly can eve
achieve greatly."
—Robert F. Kenned

MONEY

Once you learn that you can't pay your credit card with your credit card, your financial education soars. So it is with training, which demands a similar high-level budgeting, albeit around time and energy, not cash. Running requires both strength and endurance, yet the time invested in one steals from the other. Worse, they vie for your body's best abilities.

Strength training delivers speed to your cheerful legs, even if you don't give tuppence about being fast. Its exuberance alone delivers in smiles. Besides, you need these muscles for hills and for consistent pacing. They have side benefits as well. Strength training increases bone density and relieves symptoms of arthritis. Because muscle is more dense than fat, it requires more energy to sustain. Strong people burn more calories (helping them lose weight, if that's the goal).

Its rival, endurance training, forestalls all manner of heart problems. It improves circulation and reduces the risk of diabetes, breast and colon cancer, arthritis, and depression. Most important, it is central to any running program, the favored child. Plenty of weak runners can plod through seven miles. But unless you've built the endurance, both in running muscles and in cardiovascular fitness, a sprint down the block to catch a bus will leave you gasping and perhaps a little embarrassed.

Physiologically, the difference comes down to two essential types of muscle fiber: fast-twitch (speed) and slow-twitch (endurance). Build up one at the cost of the other.

While this is generally true, the human animal is more acute at accountancy. You already know whether your body is better suited to speed or distance—as well as the tradeoffs. So with weaknesses identified and goals adjusted, your training program is perfectly budgeted, right?

Not so fast. The perfect balance of strength and endurance training will change over time and will change your expectations along with it. If you run to maintain weight, strength training is all but mandatory. But once extra pounds begin to melt, increased mileage takes you to your magic number. When training for a distance event, endurance drives you to the starting line. Still, dedicate some workouts to speed in the weeks leading up to your taper, and your race-day performance will likely surprise you. Over the years, older runners tend to neglect strength training, yet muscle mass is the first thing aging steals from us.

It's easy enough to stir up the proper mix in weekly workouts (add weights or resistance machines to round off accounting errors). You won't regret it. Unfortunately, you won't get the most from what each muscle type offers. A little budgetary strategy in your weekly workouts keeps both accounts flush. The secret is to bring them up for review on a regular basis. Yes, audit your workouts and rebalance the time committed to both speed and endurance. If you're dissatisfied with either the effort or the results, it's time to review your goals. ∎

28 Monday 8

Where & When: **Distance:**

Comments:

29 Tuesday 8

Where & When: **Distance:**

Comments:

30 Wednesday 9

Where & When: **Distance:**

Comments:

31 Thursday 9

Where & When: **Distance:**

Comments:

1 Friday 9.

Where & When: **Distance:**

Comments:

March/April

Saturday 2

Where & When: Distance:

Comments:

Sunday 3

Where & When: Distance:

Comments:

© Roy Morsch/maXximages.com

tip: When bumping up weekly mileage, add frequency of workouts before tacking on longer workouts.

Distance this week: Weight:

Distance carried forward:

4 Monday
9

Where & When: **Distance:**

Comments:

5 Tuesday
9

Where & When: **Distance:**

Comments:

6 Wednesday
9

Where & When: **Distance:**

Comments:

7 Thursday
98

Where & When: **Distance:**

Comments:

8 Friday
99

Where & When: **Distance:**

Comments:

April

Saturday 9

00

Where & When: _____ Distance: _____

Comments: _____

Sunday 10

01

Where & When: _____ Distance: _____

Comments: _____

© Pete Saloutos/maXximages.com

tip: Even when it's not quite cold enough to bother with, bring a winter shell. Gusts can unexpectedly turn you into a popsicle.

Distance this week: _____ Weight: _____

Distance carried forward:

11 Monday   10

Where & When: Distance:
Comments:

12 Tuesday   10

Where & When: Distance:
Comments:

13 Wednesday   10

Where & When: Distance:
Comments:

14 Thursday   10

Where & When: Distance:
Comments:

15 Friday   10

Where & When: Distance:
Comments:

April

07

here & When: Distance:

omments:

08   **Sunday 17**

here & When: Distance:

omments:

© Yellowdog/maXximages.com

tip: On a treadmill, feet tend to move up and down, without the forward propulsion required on pavement. To compensate, dial up a little incline.

istance this week: Weight:

18 Monday   10

Where & When: Distance:

Comments:

19 Tuesday   11

Where & When: Distance:

Comments:

20 Wednesday   1

Where & When: Distance:

Comments:

21 Thursday   11

Where & When: Distance:

Comments:

22 Friday   11

Where & When: Distance:

Comments:

April

Saturday 23

Where & When: Distance:
Comments:

Sunday 24

Where & When: Distance:
Comments:

© George Shelley/maXximages.com

tip: Is it okay to run seven days a week? Yes, but make sure three of those days are very easy workouts.

Distance this week: Weight:

25 Monday   11

Where & When: **Distance:**

Comments:

26 Tuesday   11

Where & When: **Distance:**

Comments:

27 Wednesday   11

Where & When: **Distance:**

Comments:

28 Thursday   11

Where & When: **Distance:**

Comments:

29 Friday   12

Where & When: **Distance:**

Comments:

Saturday 30

1

here & When: Distance:

mments:

Sunday 1

2

here & When: Distance:

mments:

" run 17 miles every morning. People ask me how
keep my teeth from chattering in the wintertime.
leave them in the locker."

–Walt Stack, who starred in Nike's first "Just Do It" commercial in 1988

tip: Never take ibuprofen before a workout. Many runners use it to preemptively stop muscle soreness. But with the intensity of a workout, it can cause permanent damage to kidneys and the gastrointestinal system.

tes:

stance this week: Weight:

May

SUNDAY	MONDAY	TUESDAY	WEDNESDAY	THURSDAY	FRIDAY	SATURDAY
1 Easter (Orthodox)	2 May Day (Australia—NT) Early May Bank Holiday (Ireland, UK)	3	4	5	6	7
8 Mother's Day (USA, Australia, Canada, NZ)	9	10	11	12	13	14
15	16	17	18	19	20	21 Armed Forces Day (U⁹
22	23 Victoria Day (Canada)	24	25	26	27	28
29	30 Memorial Day (USA) Spring Bank Holiday (UK)	31				

"Winning isn't everything,
but wanting to win is.

—Vince Lombar

MIRTH

There are two kinds of runners—no, make that three. Fifteen minutes into a sour workout, when it's clear that energy and purpose have evaporated, the first runner pushes through it, sometimes finding a breakthrough in the desultory boredom, sometimes not. The second runner quits. Disgust and cynicism brew in the hours afterward. It usually takes a night's sleep before resolve returns. The third runner changes the workout.

Most of us have been all three of these at one time or another. A good case can be made for them all. Use the bad run under foot to reflect. Be suspicious of cheap rationalizations and places to hide from yourself. How you react might say something about your character, but it reveals even more about your training program. Rejigger or rethink yourself.

The plodder typically holds a goal tied closely to the calendar, and there is proven wisdom in pushing yourself onward, no matter what, when a glaring bathroom scale or a race date looms. So plod, but accept the occasional defeat with mercy . . . for yourself. Sometimes it simply makes sense to quit a bad run, no need to feel guilty or diminished by it. Guilt has absolutely no purpose in training. And the comfort of commitment to a routine can backfire. To be satisfied simply by sticking to a plan dodges its purpose. To be sure, you won't progress without consistency and discipline. But these don't yield results by themselves.

Quitters hate themselves in the moment (never shame them), and they too often let the self-inflicted insult linger. This is a mistake. If your heart isn't in a workout, you can't expect to reap much from it. You don't have to defend quitting. You feel weak or unfocused, a friend invites you out for a drink, or the freezing rain douses ambition. Call these excuses, if you like, but don't belittle yourself over them. Remember that you're in charge of your training program, not the other way around. The trouble with quitting is that it's habit-forming. Goals crash on these seemingly unthreatening rocks.

We'd all love the ingenious courage that improves a workout going badly. Here's one way to squirrel up the nerve: Abandon expectations, embrace what feels good or brings satisfaction, and throw everything into it. It's a great case for cross training, but also for switching to a trail or track, working a short session of hard hill charges, or descending into the basement for that dust-covered treadmill you haven't visited in months. However you improvise, remember that it's a diversion from big-picture goals. Sometimes the benefits educate or surprise; more often they simply burn calories and a little time. Occasionally they humiliate.

Bum workouts are inevitable, of course, and the worst of them poison your self-confidence. So head them off with a strategy: Plod, quit, or change. Just don't act too fast. An aimless run sometimes holds the mysterious power to swell your heart, locomotive-like. But don't read too much into it. Hell, it's just a workout. ■

Distance carried forward:

2 Monday   12

Where & When: **Distance:**
Comments:

3 Tuesday   12

Where & When: **Distance:**
Comments:

4 Wednesday   12

Where & When: **Distance:**
Comments:

5 Thursday   12

Where & When: **Distance:**
Comments:

6 Friday   12

Where & When: **Distance:**
Comments:

May

Saturday 7

28

here & When: Distance:

omments:

29

Sunday 8

here & When: Distance:

omments:

tip: On trails, effort rather than pace tells you how hard you have worked. Your times will be slower than on pavement. So enjoy the splendor of the surroundings.

© Michael Reusse/maXximages.com

istance this week: **Weight:**

Distance carried forward:

9 Monday 13

Where & When: **Distance:**
Comments:

10 Tuesday 13

Where & When: **Distance:**
Comments:

11 Wednesday 13

Where & When: **Distance:**
Comments:

12 Thursday 13

Where & When: **Distance:**
Comments:

13 Friday 13

Where & When: **Distance:**
Comments:

55

Saturday 14

here & When: Distance:

omments:

56

Sunday 15

here & When: Distance:

omments:

© J.M. Guyon/maXximages.com

tip: Forty miles per week is safe for the vast majority of runners. Beyond that, increase mileage slowly. The risk of injury spikes.

istance this week: Weight:

Distance carried forward:

16 Monday
13

Where & When: **Distance:**
Comments:

17 Tuesday
13

Where & When: **Distance:**
Comments:

18 Wednesday
13

Where & When: **Distance:**
Comments:

19 Thursday
14

Where & When: **Distance:**
Comments:

20 Friday
14

Where & When: **Distance:**
Comments:

Saturday 21

42

Where & When: Distance:

Comments:

Sunday 22

43

Where & When: Distance:

Comments:

© Charles Knox/maXximages.com

tip: Eating or drinking something cold before a hot workout can extend your endurance by lowering your body's core temperature.

Distance this week: Weight:

Distance carried forward:

23 Monday   144

Where & When: Distance:
Comments:

24 Tuesday   145

Where & When: Distance:
Comments:

25 Wednesday   146

Where & When: Distance:
Comments:

26 Thursday   147

Where & When: Distance:
Comments:

27 Friday   148

Where & When: Distance:
Comments:

49

Where & When: Distance:

Comments:

50

Sunday 29

Where & When: Distance:

Comments:

"Plough deep while sluggards sleep and you shall have corn to sell and to keep."

—Benjamin Franklin

tip: Compression tights may reduce muscle soreness by limiting swelling and increasing blood flow.

Notes:

Distance this week: Weight:

June

SUNDAY	MONDAY	TUESDAY	WEDNESDAY	THURSDAY	FRIDAY	SATURDAY
			1	2	3	4
5	6 Ramadan Queen's Birthday (NZ) Foundation Day (Australia—WA) Spring Bank Holiday (Ireland)	7	8	9	10	11
12	13 Queen's Birthday (Australia—except WA)	14 Flag Day (USA)	15	16	17	18
19 Father's Day (USA, Canada, Ireland, UK)	20	21	22	23	24	25
26	27	28	29	30		

*"Never was anything grea
achieved without danger."*
—Niccolò Machiavell

DOC

You live by numbers: Miles, laps, steps, calories, pounds, socks, heartbeats, months, days, seconds. There's always some new calculus for progress and defeat. And thus we count, believing in some vague way that, whatever else the numerals reveal, we are measuring assured invincibility.

This is a dangerous fiction. And in the warmer months when explosive, hard workouts beckon, it's worth looking at some arcane digits that elude your radar, but that tell you what's genuinely possible in the coming months and years. You'll find them at your doctor's office.

If you're over 25, an annual blood test should be part of your training program. Blood doesn't lie. You'll need to fast 12 hours beforehand and you should definitely skip all but a very light workout the previous day in order to avoid skewing results. Most importantly, follow up. Don't merely surrender your arm to the clinic's vampires, waiting for your doctor to call with an alarming discovery. Discuss even normal lab findings, either in person, by phone, or by e-mail.

Many runners have high cholesterol, including elite athletes. The "bad" version (LDL) clogs arteries, sabotaging blood flow, and triggering inflammation. If your diet is sensible and your weight is normal, blame your parents. Statins may help. The better solution is to raise your "good" cholesterol (HDL), which helps remove the evil stuff.

Fruits, vegetables, nuts, fish, and olive oil—you've heard it all before—can help. If not, your doctor can give you an earful. The noble act of running also raises HDL, though scientists cannot tell you how. No matter; here are the magic numbers: LDL below 100 mg/dL; HDL above 60 mg/dL.

Diabetes confounds training programs in countless ways, and again, the menace runs in families. If you've had no diagnosis (or symptoms) for it, you don't have to start worrying until you're about 45. Again, running helps fight the disease by lowering blood-sugar levels as muscles burn glucose. If in doubt, watch your magic numbers: less than 100 mg/dL.

Training saps iron from the blood, ironically, because it increases blood volume. There's less to go around. Popeye had it right for diet, and the best way to keep your levels up is by what you stuff into your maw. Still, if your performance slides, or you're feeling fatigued or achy, check your magic numbers: above 25 ng/mL.

Running proves you're alive, at least as a display. Blood pressure tells you far more about how close you stand to your grave than any other number. Better still, you don't have to surrender blood for it. Get it checked as often as opportunity allows, even at the grocery store these days. Magic numbers: under 120/80 mmHg. ■

Distance carried forward:

30 Monday   1

Where & When: **Distance:**

Comments:

31 Tuesday   15

Where & When: **Distance:**

Comments:

1 Wednesday   15

Where & When: **Distance:**

Comments:

2 Thursday   15

Where & When: **Distance:**

Comments:

3 Friday   15

Where & When: **Distance:**

Comments:

May/June

56

Saturday 4

here & When: Distance:

omments:

57

Sunday 5

here & When: Distance:

omments:

tip: Longer, low-intensity runs indeed burn more fat than short, high-intensity workouts. (Alas, they also tend to spike your appetite.)

© Noah Clayton/maXximages.com

istance this week: Weight:

6 Monday   15

Where & When: Distance:
Comments:

7 Tuesday   15

Where & When: Distance:
Comments:

8 Wednesday   16

Where & When: Distance:
Comments:

9 Thursday   16

Where & When: Distance:
Comments:

10 Friday   16

Where & When: Distance:
Comments:

June

Saturday 11

3

ere & When: Distance:

mments:

Sunday 12

4

ere & When: Distance:

mments:

© Erik Isakson/maXximages.com

tip: For controlling blood sugar, multiple short workouts throughout the day are more effective than one daily long run.

tance this week: Weight:

13 Monday
16

Where & When: Distance:

Comments:

14 Tuesday
16

Where & When: Distance:

Comments:

15 Wednesday
16

Where & When: Distance:

Comments:

16 Thursday
16

Where & When: Distance:

Comments:

17 Friday
16

Where & When: Distance:

Comments:

June

Saturday 18

o

_____

_____

_____

ere & When: _____   Distance: _____

mments: _____

Sunday 19

1

_____

_____

ere & When: _____   Distance: _____

mments: _____

© Michael DeYoung/maXximages.com

ip: Physical inactivity is the greatest contributor to heart disease for women over 30.

stance this week: _____   Weight: _____

Distance carried forward: _____

20 Monday 1̲7̲

_____
_____
_____

Where & When: _____ **Distance:** _____
Comments: _____

21 Tuesday 1̲7̲

_____
_____
_____

Where & When: _____ **Distance:** _____
Comments: _____

22 Wednesday 1̲7̲

_____
_____
_____

Where & When: _____ **Distance:** _____
Comments: _____

23 Thursday 1̲7̲

_____
_____
_____

Where & When: _____ **Distance:** _____
Comments: _____

24 Friday 1̲7̲

_____
_____
_____

Where & When: _____ **Distance:** _____
Comments: _____

June

Saturday 25

'7

_____

here & When: **Distance:**

mments:

Sunday 26

'8

_____

here & When: **Distance:**

mments:

"Methinks that the moment my legs begin to move, my thoughts begin to flow. Only while we are in action is the circulation perfect."

—Henry David Thoreau

tip: Add a foam roller to your running gear for a post-workout massage. It feels great, builds strength and stability, and you can listen to music or watch TV while using it.

tes:

_____

stance this week: **Weight:**

July

SUNDAY	MONDAY	TUESDAY	WEDNESDAY	THURSDAY	FRIDAY	SATURDAY
					1	2
					Canada Day	
3	4	5	6	7	8	9
	Independence Day (USA)	Eid al-Fitr				
10	11	12	13	14	15	16
17	18	19	20	21	22	23
24	25	26	27	28	29	30
31						

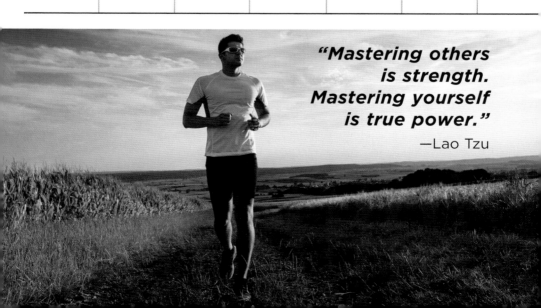

"Mastering others is strength. Mastering yourself is true power."
—Lao Tzu

TORPOR

Would that we were fire. A quart of cold sports drink, ice water poured over the head, 30 minutes sitting shaded, semi-nude, with a wet towel around our necks—we believe we can defeat heat as easily as extinguishing an ember. We are wrong.

Heat is slow and stealthy. The greatest danger runners face during the sweltering months is the deception that our own bodies make reliable thermometers for danger. Sensory relief brings false assurance. With thirst slaked and heart settled to a familiar resting rate, we head back into the sun, coast clear.

Except that it's not. The predator still stalks us. Hot weather kills more Americans than any other type of natural disaster. Thousands more die from illnesses made worse by heat, often attributed to natural causes such as heart attacks or kidney disease. And heaven knows how many people are stricken, but survive, their numbers never reported. Most of us succumb, not when temperatures spike, but toward the end of a heat wave—days, even weeks, into a hot-weather training program. Most vulnerable are the elderly and athletes.

It's not hard to see why. The body functions within a narrow temperature range. Above 105 degrees F, enzymes break down, disrupting normal metabolic processes. Death comes knocking. Blood vessels are your body's internal radiator. When you get hot, they dilate to cool your core temperature. These pipes don't dilate as readily in the elderly. Runners who haven't acclimatized to the simmering weather haven't built enough store of blood plasma—typically 10 days to two weeks—for dilation to be effective.

Sweat is even more important for cooling. As it pours forth, it evaporates, which draws heat from the body. So the tanks need to be full. Both athletes and elderly are prone to dehydration for different reasons. Saturating sweat glands requires hours, long after thirst has passed. Likewise, diuretic drugs that leech hydration can take days to metabolize. Betablockers, antidepressants, antihistamines, and anticholinergics contribute to dehydration. Contrary to popular belief, alcohol takes more than 24 hours to make a complete exit. Needless to say, cocaine and methamphetamine work against you when you're training under a blazing sun.

Whether you're trying to purge your body of chemicals that raise the risks of heat illnesses or building the bodily juices that keep you cool, take it slow. Throughout the day, keep a glass of water within reach (in winter, too). Add miles to your workouts gradually, and curtail them immediately if you feel dizziness, sudden weakness, headache, nausea, or muscle cramps. Seek shelter. Summer is long and enjoyable. There's no need to rush it. ■

Distance carried forward:

27 Monday
17

Where & When: **Distance:**

Comments:

28 Tuesday
18

Where & When: **Distance:**

Comments:

29 Wednesday
18

Where & When: **Distance:**

Comments:

30 Thursday
18

Where & When: **Distance:**

Comments:

1 Friday
18

Where & When: **Distance:**

Comments:

June/July

Saturday 2

here & When: Distance:

omments:

Sunday 3

here & When: Distance:

omments:

© Matt Dutile/maXximages.com

tip: For distance events, rehearse your hydration strategy as keenly as you rehearse pacing.

istance this week: Weight:

Distance carried forward:

4 Monday   18

Where & When: **Distance:**

Comments:

5 Tuesday   18

Where & When: **Distance:**

Comments:

6 Wednesday   18

Where & When: **Distance:**

Comments:

7 Thursday   18

Where & When: **Distance:**

Comments:

8 Friday   19

Where & When: **Distance:**

Comments:

July

Saturday 9

here & When: Distance:

omments:

Sunday 10

here & When: Distance:

omments:

tip: If your legs feel heavy on race day, chances are you didn't taper sufficiently.

© Tim Kiusalaas/maXximages.com

istance this week: Weight:

Distance carried forward:

11 Monday 19

Where & When: **Distance:**

Comments:

12 Tuesday 19

Where & When: **Distance:**

Comments:

13 Wednesday 19

Where & When: **Distance:**

Comments:

14 Thursday 19

Where & When: **Distance:**

Comments:

15 Friday 19

Where & When: **Distance:**

Comments:

July

Saturday 16

8

here & When: Distance:

omments:

99

Sunday 17

here & When: Distance:

omments:

© Michael DeYoung/maXximages.com

tip: Try grass. The softer surface makes your hams and core muscles work harder with less punishing impact.

istance this week: Weight:

18 Monday   20

Where & When: Distance:

Comments:

19 Tuesday   20

Where & When: Distance:

Comments:

20 Wednesday   20

Where & When: Distance:

Comments:

21 Thursday   20

Where & When: Distance:

Comments:

22 Friday   20

Where & When: Distance:

Comments:

July

Saturday 23

)5

here & When: _____ Distance: _____

omments: _____

Sunday 24

)6

here & When: _____ Distance: _____

omments: _____

© Jordan Siemens/maXximages.com

ip: The rising popularity of running back-to-back events poses no specific danger. But your goals for each race should be entirely different.

stance this week: _____ Weight: _____

25 Monday   20

Where & When: **Distance:**

Comments:

26 Tuesday   20

Where & When: **Distance:**

Comments:

27 Wednesday   20

Where & When: **Distance:**

Comments:

28 Thursday   21

Where & When: **Distance:**

Comments:

29 Friday   2

Where & When: **Distance:**

Comments:

July

Saturday 30

2

ere & When: Distance:

mments:

Sunday 31

3

ere & When: Distance:

mments:

"ou have to do it for no ulterior motive. You have to do it for the thing itself."

-Frank Shorter, American former long-distance runner who won the gold medal in the marathon at the 1972 Summer Olympics

tip: Bank sleep. The night before a big event is commonly restless. It won't hurt your performance, but try to sleep deep and long in the days leading up to a race.

tes:

tance this week: Weight:

August

SUNDAY	MONDAY	TUESDAY	WEDNESDAY	THURSDAY	FRIDAY	SATURDAY
	1 Summer Bank Holiday (Ireland, UK—Scotland, Australia—NSW) Picnic Day (Australia—NT)	2	3	4	5	6
7	8	9	10	11	12	13
14	15	16	17	18	19	20
21	22	23	24	25	26	27
28	29 Summer Bank Holiday (UK—except Scotland)	30	31			

"Every calamity is a spur and a valuable hint."
—Ralph Waldo Emerson

ADAPT

Astronaut Sunita Williams completed her first Nautica Malibu Triathlon from the International Space Station, 240 miles above her earthling competitors. When he grew bored with the gym in the offshore oil rig where he worked, Derek Cooper ran laps around the helicopter landing pad (22 to the mile), and qualified for the Hermann Ironman Texas event. Keith Fouts finished a marathon at the South Pole in balmy minus-25-degree weather.

So how have you proven your moxie lately? Running produces all manner of daredevils and whack jobs, of course, but high summer should lead us all to reconsider not only the limitations and adaptations of training, but also the boundless possibilities. It should likewise let us indulge a little eccentricity.

First pull out your topographic map. Folks who live at higher elevations develop abilities coastal flatlanders lack. Thinner air means less oxygen reaches muscles. Over time, the body produces more red blood cells to compensate, which increases VO2 max rate. When they descend to sea levels, most Rocky Mountain runners working at the same intensity as Kansans or Floridians can kick their rumps. To stay competitive with mountain folk, endurance matters. Add miles to your workouts.

Hilly terrain makes different demands and serves up speed as its reward. Never be dismissive of speed. It carries you over a finish line when you are physically and morally depleted or through a muddy path when you hate your workout, hate the world. It shows up uninvited, like an old college roommate whose presence you greet with both resentment and trust. You don't need hills to build it. Speed drills themselves do the trick, and unlike physical inclines, drills let you methodically control your progress.

Then there's climate. Shudder, if you must, when frigid air envelops you at the doorstep (ye intrepid runner). It takes only minutes for the inner furnace to kick in. Cold-weather runners obviously need to plan, especially for clothing layers. Still, unpleasant shock typically outweighs actual danger. On the other hand, adapting to hot weather is a slow and treacherous tango—a dance with a tarantula in a tuxedo. Keep this in mind whenever you board an airplane for an uncustomary hot destination. Again, it takes *weeks* to acclimate.

Mental adaptations present a different quandary. Brain and body both sabotage and rescue each other. We've all known the liberation a hard workout brings to an exhausted mind. Many creative breakthroughs (and some salvaged relationships) come from pounding the pavement. Perhaps the magic lies in the distraction alone, a chance for neurons to rejuvenate, exertion and repetitive motion opening a window for fresh thinking. It's also true that any exercise feels harder when you're coming to it all burned out, overlong attention focused on things that don't matter. Studies show that endurance is compromised. Your job is to force exhausted body and exhausted mind to somehow work together. Get to it. ∎

Distance carried forward:

1 Monday 21

Where & When: **Distance:**

Comments:

2 Tuesday 2

Where & When: **Distance:**

Comments:

3 Wednesday 2

Where & When: **Distance:**

Comments:

4 Thursday 2

Where & When: **Distance:**

Comments:

5 Friday 2

Where & When: **Distance:**

Comments:

August

Saturday 6

19

here & When: Distance:

mments:

20

Sunday 7

here & When: Distance:

mments:

© David Foster/maXximages.com

ip: At the starting gun, wait until the corral thins out before turning on your headphones. Don't become the oblivious speed bump everyone delights to watch fall.

stance this week: Weight:

8 Monday   2

Where & When: Distance:
Comments:

9 Tuesday   22

Where & When: Distance:
Comments:

10 Wednesday   22

Where & When: Distance:
Comments:

11 Thursday   22

Where & When: Distance:
Comments:

12 Friday   22

Where & When: Distance:
Comments:

Saturday 13

26

here & When: Distance:

Comments:

Sunday 14

27

here & When: Distance:

Comments:

© Himsl Leo/maXximages.com

tip: Purchase motivation. New running shoes, a wearable workout monitor, or a paid race-registration fee pump surprising energy into tired training routines.

Distance this week: Weight:

15 Monday 22

Where & When: Distance:

Comments:

16 Tuesday 22

Where & When: Distance:

Comments:

17 Wednesday 23

Where & When: Distance:

Comments:

18 Thursday 23

Where & When: Distance:

Comments:

19 Friday 23

Where & When: Distance:

Comments:

August

Saturday 20

33

here & When: Distance:

omments:

Sunday 21

34

here & When: Distance:

omments:

© Henn Photography/maXximages.

tip: If you're worried about "hitting the wall" in a marathon, you will. Fill your workouts with visions of what lies beyond it.

istance this week: Weight:

Distance carried forward: _____

22 Monday   23

_____
_____
_____

Where & When: _____ **Distance:** _____
Comments: _____
_____

23 Tuesday   23

_____
_____
_____

Where & When: _____ **Distance:** _____
Comments: _____
_____

24 Wednesday   23

_____
_____
_____

Where & When: _____ **Distance:** _____
Comments: _____
_____

25 Thursday   23

_____
_____
_____

Where & When: _____ **Distance:** _____
Comments: _____
_____

26 Friday   23

_____
_____
_____

Where & When: _____ **Distance:** _____
Comments: _____
_____

August

Saturday 27

40

Where & When: Distance:

Comments:

Sunday 28

41

Where & When: Distance:

Comments:

"Desire, both the whispers and the shouts, is the map we have been given to find the only life worth living."

—John Eldredge

tip: Slather on sunscreen thick and often. Just because your skin hasn't reddened doesn't mean the sun isn't permanently damaging it.

Notes:

Distance this week: Weight:

September

SUNDAY	MONDAY	TUESDAY	WEDNESDAY	THURSDAY	FRIDAY	SATURDAY
				1	2	3
4	5	6	7	8	9	10
Father's Day (Australia, NZ)	Labor Day (USA, Canada)					
11	12	13	14	15	16	17
Eid al-Adha						
18	19	20	21	22	23	24
			U.N. International Day of Peace			
25	26	27	28	29	30	
	Queen's Birthday (Australia—WA)					

"A goal is a dream with a deadline."

—Napoleon Hill

TERRAIN

The great thing about Planet Earth is there's so much of it. So why do we confine our customary workouts to a tiny, trodden swath? It's familiar, that's why. It delivers a credible way to measure progress both in speed and distance. Yet it likewise limits these things.

When we seek new challenges in our workouts, we tend to use visual references—adding hills or an extended mile through the park. We rarely consider what's underfoot. The ground that greets our feet provides the best platform for bringing about improvement. It's also a laboratory, because there is no ideal surface for running. Your age, stride, previous injuries, and prayerful goals make the whole business unique. Besides, your foot is a complicated convergence of bones, muscles, and ligaments.

So you'll have to find your own perfect terrain. Sports physiologists recommend variation, if not in a single workout, then throughout the week. This is an excellent case for adding the occasional trail run to your normal brew, especially if you know an off-road path with hard and soft surfaces, sand, loose gravel, and other assorted challenges. These strengthen not only your feet but every muscle group that extends upward into the back of your neck.

And yes, trail running increases the risk of injury. You'll have to slow your pace, shorten your stride. Divert your attention from the road ahead to where each step falls. However, the common wisdom that softer ground puts less stress on your body is receding, and with it, the notion that thicker padding in running shoes reduces injury.

Evidence on these matters cuts both ways. You'll have to find out for yourself.

This much we know: Concrete is harder than asphalt, rocks and dried mud are harder than sand, and today's state-of-the-art running tracks are akin to heaven for the relief they offer feet, ankles, knees, and hips. Harder surfaces produce greater speed and distance, but can also torture (any middle-aged runner returning from a 3:00 a.m. bathroom trip the night after a workout on a city sidewalk can report the difference).

With hard surfaces, your legs and hips instinctively bend with each step to absorb the shock. This is returned in forward propulsion, i.e., speed and distance. Consider yourself a basketball. World records don't fall from marathons run on the beach. With harder surfaces, the efficiency of each step soars . . . especially if it's an unfailing hard surface. Both progress and danger lie in the mystery of uncertain terrain.

The more serious trouble lies not with changing stiffness underfoot, but with traction. Wet grass, slick mud, and gravel cause far more sprains and pulled calves than predictable pounding. How firma is your terra? You'll have to sort it out. The only availing consensus is that varied terrain makes you stronger. Keep in mind that terrain changes even within each footfall. Landing, then pushing off from different gradations (or with random rocks jabbing at your feet) should heighten awareness about the task at hand. They keep both head and feet on the ground. ∎

Distance carried forward:

29 Monday 24

Where & When: Distance:
Comments:

30 Tuesday 24

Where & When: Distance:
Comments:

31 Wednesday 24

Where & When: Distance:
Comments:

1 Thursday 24

Where & When: Distance:
Comments:

2 Friday 24

Where & When: Distance:
Comments:

Aug/Sept

47

Saturday 3

here & When: _____ Distance: _____

mments: _____

48

Sunday 4

here & When: _____ Distance: _____

mments: _____

© Johnér RF/maXximages.com

ip: Need to work hills, but none to be found where you live? Embanked overpasses, parking garages, treadmills, and stadium steps all do the trick.

stance this week: _____ Weight: _____

Distance carried forward: _____

5 Monday   24

_____
_____
_____

Where & When: _____   **Distance:** _____
Comments: _____
_____

6 Tuesday   25

_____
_____
_____

Where & When: _____   **Distance:** _____
Comments: _____
_____

7 Wednesday   2!

_____
_____
_____

Where & When: _____   **Distance:** _____
Comments: _____
_____

8 Thursday   25

_____
_____
_____

Where & When: _____   **Distance:** _____
Comments: _____
_____

9 Friday   25

_____
_____
_____

Where & When: _____   **Distance:** _____
Comments: _____
_____

September

Saturday 10

4

ere & When: Distance:

mments:

Sunday 11

5

ere & When: Distance:

mments:

p: Even on race day, be willing to improvise.

tance this week: Weight:

12 Monday   2

Where & When: Distance:
Comments:

13 Tuesday   2

Where & When: Distance:
Comments:

14 Wednesday   2

Where & When: Distance:
Comments:

15 Thursday   2

Where & When: Distance:
Comments:

16 Friday   2

Where & When: Distance:
Comments:

September

Saturday 17

1

Where & When: _____   Distance: _____

Comments:

Sunday 18

2

Where & When: _____   Distance: _____

Comments:

Tip: All runners need speed work, but you needn't go at it like math. In the middle of your long run, put on a burst of speed for a few seconds, and then slow down until you recover. Repeat.

Distance this week: _____   Weight: _____

Distance carried forward: _____

19 Monday   2(

_____

_____

_____

Where & When: _____ **Distance:** _____

Comments: _____

_____

20 Tuesday   2(

_____

_____

_____

Where & When: _____ **Distance:** _____

Comments: _____

_____

21 Wednesday   2(

_____

_____

_____

Where & When: _____ **Distance:** _____

Comments: _____

_____

22 Thursday   2(

_____

_____

_____

Where & When: _____ **Distance:** _____

Comments: _____

_____

23 Friday   2(

_____

_____

_____

Where & When: _____ **Distance:** _____

Comments: _____

_____

September

Saturday 24

8

ere & When: _____ Distance: _____

mments: _____

Sunday 25

9

ere & When: _____ Distance: _____

mments: _____

© Sam Edwards/maXximages.com

ip: Learn from NASCAR. Drafting saves fuel—even for runners. When you're fatigued, duck behind another runner, especially in a headwind.

stance this week: _____ Weight: _____

Distance carried forward:

26 Monday
2

Where & When: **Distance:**
Comments:

27 Tuesday
2

Where & When: **Distance:**
Comments:

28 Wednesday
2

Where & When: **Distance:**
Comments:

29 Thursday
2

Where & When: **Distance:**
Comments:

30 Friday
2

Where & When: **Distance:**
Comments:

Sept/Oct

Saturday 1

75

here & When: _____ Distance: _____

omments: _____

Sunday 2

76

here & When: _____ Distance: _____

omments: _____

"Pick battles big enough to matter, small enough to win."

—Jonathan Kozol

tip: When running after dark, lose the headphones and always carry ID.

Notes: _____

Distance this week: _____ Weight: _____

SUNDAY	MONDAY	TUESDAY	WEDNESDAY	THURSDAY	FRIDAY	SATURDA
						1
2	3	4	5	6	7	8
	Rosh Hashanah* Labour Day (Australia—ACT, SA, NSW, QLD)	Rosh Hashanah ends				
9	10	11	12	13	14	15
	Columbus Day (USA) Thanksgiving (Canada)		Yom Kippur*			
16	17	18	19	20	21	22
23	24	25	26	27	28	29
	United Nations Day Labour Day (NZ)					
30	31					
	Halloween Bank Holiday (Ireland)					

*Begins at sundown the previous day

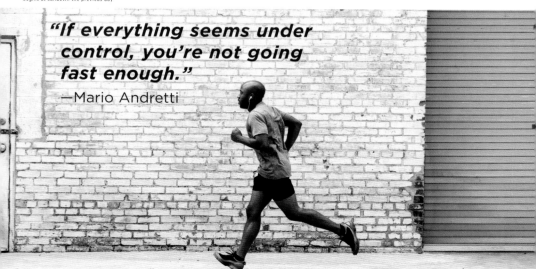

"**If everything seems under control, you're not going fast enough.**"
—Mario Andretti

SKELETON

If nothing hurts in the morning, you might be dead. Runners have a vast repertoire of aches, the passing slights of hard-earned miles, of life itself. Yet when agony lingers—or worse, when it pronounces lasting disability—the music stops. Acute injury needs no prognosis on your part. Ripping pain, blood, immobility, vomiting, or loss of consciousness all issue their own directives.

Other tortures require contemplation. Muscles heal on their own, slowly and with recurring grudges. They are stupid, but loyal donkeys. Lighten their loads far longer than seems reasonable. Pain tells you little about how much they've healed. Have sympathy for them. They propel you, even though they will bite you on the bum if you become overeager in recovery.

The pivot points of our skeletons present an entirely different frame for decisions. Feet, ankles, knees, hips, lower back, shoulders, and neck all beg for specific remedies when they hurt. Sports medicine, forever advancing, offers at best a Boy Scout bromide as advice: Avoid injury. Unless you've got a better idea, this might be the only way to scare off a permanent limp.

It seems we will never know if stretching before a workout prevents injuries to these hinges beneath our flesh. The subject has been studied to death, and the evidence is inconclusively gaseous. There's more to be said for the benefits of stretching *after* a workout, though anyone who offers specific advice in this matter is probably trying to sell you something.

It's irrefutable that a warm-up helps ward off injury. The evidence is vast. Light loads to the various hoists and bending parts pump blood to the muscles that support them, increasing their elasticity, allowing them to do their jobs better (they also safely prime the heart and lungs for serious work). Warm muscles contract more forcefully and relax more quickly. They extend range of motion. They lessen the likelihood of strains. And they rehearse your various reflexes for landing, leaping, darting, and other actions that your workout demands.

Every step you take—even on a treadmill—requires a unique dance of balance, strength, anticipation, urgency, and lucky guesses. In fact, it's this so-called neuromuscular training that has captivated the recent attention of sports physiologists. Growing evidence shows that it prevents all manner of injuries to joints and tendons, especially the dreaded ruptured anterior cruciate ligament (runner's knee), which is extremely painful and can put you on a surgery gurney, with many months to recuperate. Any Internet search turns up dozens of drills and exercise programs that train muscles and mind to protect your joints. Most involve 15 to 20 minutes of marching, jumping, squatting, side-to-side shuffling, and the like.

Because your body's architecture is unique, you'll have to decide which of these best protects your dancing skeleton. Should they fail, injury may require a second, sometimes third, opinion. Be skeptical about back and knee surgery; these are often useless and expensive. Lowered expectations and patience usually work better. Trust your bones' own abilities to mend. ∎

Distance carried forward: _____

3 Monday   2̄

_____
_____
_____

Where & When: _____   **Distance:** _____
Comments: _____
_____

4 Tuesday   2̄

_____
_____
_____

Where & When: _____   **Distance:** _____
Comments: _____
_____

5 Wednesday   2̄

_____
_____
_____

Where & When: _____   **Distance:** _____
Comments: _____
_____

6 Thursday   28

_____
_____
_____

Where & When: _____   **Distance:** _____
Comments: _____
_____

7 Friday   28

_____
_____
_____

Where & When: _____   **Distance:** _____
Comments: _____
_____

October

Saturday 8

82

Where & When: _____ Distance: _____

Comments: _____

Sunday 9

83

Where & When: _____ Distance: _____

Comments: _____

© Yosuke Tanaka/maXximages.com

tip: Pump those arms! Yes, the effort burns energy your legs would rather use. But arm swing reduces overall metabolic costs by helping you maintain balance in motion and by increasing forward propulsion.

Distance this week: _____ Weight: _____

Distance carried forward: _____

10 Monday   28

_____
_____
_____

Where & When: _____ **Distance:** _____
Comments: _____
_____

11 Tuesday   28

_____
_____
_____

Where & When: _____ **Distance:** _____
Comments: _____
_____

12 Wednesday   28

_____
_____
_____

Where & When: _____ **Distance:** _____
Comments: _____
_____

13 Thursday   28

_____
_____
_____

Where & When: _____ **Distance:** _____
Comments: _____
_____

14 Friday   28

_____
_____
_____

Where & When: _____ **Distance:** _____
Comments: _____
_____

October

Saturday 15

here & When: Distance:

mments:

Sunday 16

here & When: Distance:

mments:

© Radius Images/maXximages.com

:ip: Bluetooth headphones banish the wires that pipe tunes to your ears, but your body's movement may interfere with transmission. Shop for a player that straps to your arm.

stance this week: **Weight:**

Distance carried forward:

17 Monday 29

Where & When: **Distance:**

Comments:

18 Tuesday 29

Where & When: **Distance:**

Comments:

19 Wednesday 29

Where & When: **Distance:**

Comments:

20 Thursday 29

Where & When: **Distance:**

Comments:

21 Friday 29

Where & When: **Distance:**

Comments:

October

Saturday 22

6

ere & When: _____ Distance: _____

mments: _____

7

Sunday 23

ere & When: _____ Distance: _____

mments: _____

© Yew! Images/maXximages.com

ip: At least three times a year, shed all gadgets for your workout—heart-rate monitors, calorie counters, GPSs, headphones—everything. Listen only to what your body tells you.

stance this week: _____ Weight: _____

Distance carried forward:

24 Monday
29

Where & When: **Distance:**

Comments:

25 Tuesday
29

Where & When: **Distance:**

Comments:

26 Wednesday
30

Where & When: **Distance:**

Comments:

27 Thursday
30

Where & When: **Distance:**

Comments:

28 Friday
30

Where & When: **Distance:**

Comments:

October

3

_ere & When: _____ Distance: _____

mments: _____

4

_ere & When: _____ Distance: _____

mments: _____

_Once you have proficiency in a routine, you'll no
longer experience new gains in fitness. You've got to
add different elements of stress."_

—Terrence Mahon, Mammoth Track Club coach of Deena Kastor and Anna Pierce

tip: Countermand the experts. Physical therapy is a nuanced
practice. If your orthopedist gives up on your full recovery
from a running injury, seek a second opinion.

tes: _____

_____

_____

_____

_____

stance this week: _____ **Weight:** _____

Novembe

SUNDAY	MONDAY	TUESDAY	WEDNESDAY	THURSDAY	FRIDAY	SATURDA
		1	2	3	4	5
6	7	8	9	10	11	12
		Election Day (USA)			Veterans' Day (USA) Remembrance Day (Canada, Ireland, UK)	
13	14	15	16	17	18	19
20	21	22	23	24	25	26
				Thanksgiving (USA)		
27	28	29	30			
			St. Andrew's Day (UK)			

*"A champion is someor
who gets up when he can't*

—Jack Demps

GOLDILOCKS

Let's look at the *really* big picture—your life—as in days and workouts left. How much can running raise those numbers?

A life-insurance salesperson could tell you more than a sports physiologist. Still, lots of scientific noses have burrowed into the subject. Even if you only care about next month's 10K race, or squeezing La Blanca swimsuit around your body's contours by next spring, you must sometimes wonder, what does training buy, ultimately?

Here's what we know: Runners live longer, suffer fewer chronic illnesses, and recover from almost any mortal insult, mental or physical, faster than those who can't tear themselves away from a digital screen. Beyond that, it's your best guess. In the very broadest brushstroke, you can expect to enjoy a 19 percent lower risk of dying from any cause whatsoever than a non-runner. A lifetime of running can add some five to six years to your life, if you're a breathing American today. And at least one surprise pops from many long-term studies (some beginning as far back as 1971).

It turns out that moderate running, both in pace and weekly mileage, delivers the best results. So if your goal is to rack up as many birthdays as possible, keep it to 10 or 11 minutes per mile, and under 0 miles per week. Over the years, consistently higher levels of training bring diminishing returns and may actually shorten your life, especially if you're male.

This is hardly a prescription to heed. Individual genetics and lifestyle factors, especially a history of drinking and smoking, affect longevity with far greater force than the miles you log. Besides, few runners are consistent in their training over the course of a lifetime. By the way, longevity is not a running goal. It's a prayer.

Self-respecting goals are tied to the calendar. They demand a realistic plan and a way to measure their success. Even lifelong runners tend to leap from goal to goal—success and failure, like birthday candles, commemorating many decades of private passion, self-judgment a smoky memory. Therein lies an irony. Goals push us out the door day after day, even when arthritis flares or the weather is hostile. Yet when their calendar date passes, whatever the outcome, an abyss awaits. Goals both encourage and destroy consistency.

If you want running to help you live longer, the secret lies when you're staring into that darkness. There are endless ways to take action (or no action at all). Just make sure you've got a plan to resume. Dial down, switch routines, join a gym. However you go about it, let running quit you, not the other way around. ∎

Distance carried forward:

31 Monday 30

Where & When: **Distance:**
Comments:

1 Tuesday 30

Where & When: **Distance:**
Comments:

2 Wednesday 30

Where & When: **Distance:**
Comments:

3 Thursday 30

Where & When: **Distance:**
Comments:

4 Friday 30

Where & When: **Distance:**
Comments:

Oct/Nov

o

Saturday 5

here & When: Distance:
mments:

1

Sunday 6

here & When: Distance:
mments:

© Masakazu Watanabe/maXximages.

ip: On a crowded distance race, line up on the outside of the pack.
You will likely get up to pace sooner.

stance this week: Weight:

Distance carried forward:

7 Monday 3

Where & When: Distance:

Comments:

8 Tuesday 3

Where & When: Distance:

Comments:

9 Wednesday 31

Where & When: Distance:

Comments:

10 Thursday 31

Where & When: Distance:

Comments:

11 Friday 31

Where & When: Distance:

Comments:

November

Saturday 12

7

here & When: _____   Distance: _____

mments: _____

Sunday 13

8

here & When: _____   Distance: _____

mments: _____

© Jordan Siemens/maXximages.com

tip: On long races or workouts, zone out for the first several miles so that you're not mentally exhausted at the finish.

istance this week: _____   Weight: _____

Distance carried forward:

14 Monday 3

Where & When: Distance:
Comments:

15 Tuesday 32

Where & When: Distance:
Comments:

16 Wednesday 3

Where & When: Distance:
Comments:

17 Thursday 32

Where & When: Distance:
Comments:

18 Friday 32

Where & When: Distance:
Comments:

November

Saturday 19

24

___

here & When: Distance:

omments:

Sunday 20

25

___

here & When: Distance:

omments:

© Henn Photography/maXximages.com

tip: The old formula for calculating maximum heart rate—220 minus your age—is terribly crude, often deceptive. Don't plan your workouts (or your life) around it.

Distance this week: **Weight:**

Distance carried forward:

21 Monday   32

Where & When: **Distance:**

Comments:

22 Tuesday   32

Where & When: **Distance:**

Comments:

23 Wednesday   32

Where & When: **Distance:**

Comments:

24 Thursday   32

Where & When: **Distance:**

Comments:

25 Friday   33

Where & When: **Distance:**

Comments:

November

Saturday 26

ere & When: _____ Distance: _____

mments: _____

Sunday 27

ere & When: _____ Distance: _____

mments: _____

"You have power over your mind, not outside events. Realize this, and you will find strength."

—Marcus Aurelius

tip: A case of nerves—sleepless, no appetite, unable to focus—is normal on race day. But if you feel these things a week away, take a hard look at whether you're truly prepared.

tes: _____

stance this week: _____ Weight: _____

Decembe

SUNDAY	MONDAY	TUESDAY	WEDNESDAY	THURSDAY	FRIDAY	SATURDA
				1	2	3
4	5	6	7	8	9	10 Human Rights Day
11	12	13	14	15	16	17
18	19	20	21	22	23	24 Christmas Eve
25 Christmas Day Hanukkah*	26 Kwanzaa begins (USA) Christmas Day (observed) (Australia—NT, SA, WA) Boxing Day (Canada, NZ, UK, Australia— except ACT, NT, SA) St. Stephen's Day (Ireland)	27 Christmas Day (observed) (NZ, UK, Australia—NSW, QLD, TAS) Boxing Day (observed) (Australia—ACT, NT, VIC, WA) Proclamation Day (Australia—SA)	28	29	30	31

*Begins at sundown the previous day

"People rarely succee
unless they have fun
what they are doing.
—Dale Carneg

DELIVERANCE

You owe no one an explanation for why you run nor, for that matter, how your reasons change over time. Maybe you wanted to lose weight or to slow the insults of age, only to discover years later that you're trying to shave minutes off your marathon time. Running has helped many recover from an addiction or a broken heart. Yet when bad chapters finally pass, the serenity and focused purpose of training fill a different kind of void.

Perhaps you don't even know why you run. You needn't talk to your therapist about it, but periodic reflection sharpens the quality of your workouts, the resolve you bring to them, and how you might be undercutting your own abilities. We take endless inventory of how far we've come in training and whether tomorrow's goals are realistic. Too seldom do we contemplate why our feet are striking the pavement in the immediate moment.

You already know that running provides a way to simultaneously escape an old self and to burrow within your head. These contradictions provide clarity of self, a very specific portrait of your identity. You have to muster the courage to look at it. While doing so, can you momentarily silence the gibbering voices of achievement and failure between your ears? Instead, consider how others think about you as a runner. Does training signal that you're disciplined, ambitious, optimistic, or even mystical? Perhaps it betrays you as a misanthrope, always fleeing the company of other humans or some conjured demon.

In some workouts, all of these tell the tale. What's unassailable is that you're courageous—yes, even if you only run for escape. Don't belittle the idea. Forward progress, one step and then the next, isn't just a metaphor. If you don't know or care why you train, you know at least that it provides a fabric of consistency in your life, a reassurance. It also takes planned effort, which isn't summoned from nothing. Runners, like anyone, can lie to themselves about almost any character traits, but courage for willful change is a given. Accept it.

While you're at it, accept the ways running has changed your head. Determination is the blunt and proven force for training. You won't get anywhere without it. Still, it pays back in illogical ways. Apes, chickens, and insects run. The endeavor isn't complicated. Mysteriously, training instills self-confidence in humans. Its pain brings pleasure; its monotony makes joy. What it takes from us in any workout animates us in conversation hours afterward, in our engagement with people we care about. We live better.

So maybe you should have a chat with your therapist, after all. Introspection can be a dubious and tormented business with little to show. Most workouts should concentrate explicitly on miles and times, less so on pain and self-doubt. In the coming year, stay focused. Appreciate what you've gained, and strive to become . . . still better. In the lull, let your feet talk. The road is a good listener. ■

Distance carried forward:

28 Monday   3:

Where & When: **Distance:**

Comments:

29 Tuesday   3:

Where & When: **Distance:**

Comments:

30 Wednesday   3:

Where & When: **Distance:**

Comments:

1 Thursday   33

Where & When: **Distance:**

Comments:

2 Friday   33

Where & When: **Distance:**

Comments:

Saturday 3

38

here & When: Distance:

mments:

Sunday 4

39

here & When: Distance:

mments:

© Charlie Borland/maXximages.com

tip: If you run for health alone, two hours of moderate-paced workouts a week will give you the maximum benefit for the time invested (even so, surrender to the joy of going longer).

stance this week: **Weight:**

Distance carried forward: _____

5 Monday   34

_____

_____

_____

Where & When: _____   **Distance:** _____

Comments: _____

_____

6 Tuesday   3·

_____

_____

_____

Where & When: _____   **Distance:** _____

Comments: _____

_____

7 Wednesday   34

_____

_____

_____

Where & When: _____   **Distance:** _____

Comments: _____

_____

8 Thursday   34

_____

_____

_____

Where & When: _____   **Distance:** _____

Comments: _____

_____

9 Friday   34

_____

_____

_____

Where & When: _____   **Distance:** _____

Comments: _____

_____

December

Saturday 10

5

ere & When: _____   Distance: _____

mments: _____

Sunday 11

6

ere & When: _____   Distance: _____

mments: _____

© Brandon Sawaya/maXximages.com

tip: Bummed out by a disappointing race performance? Switch events for your next competition. Consider a relay or a trail race.

stance this week: _____   Weight: _____

12 Monday
3

Where & When: Distance:
Comments:

13 Tuesday
3

Where & When: Distance:
Comments:

14 Wednesday
3

Where & When: Distance:
Comments:

15 Thursday
3

Where & When: Distance:
Comments:

16 Friday
3

Where & When: Distance:
Comments:

December

Saturday 17

2

ere & When: _____ Distance: _____

mments: _____

Sunday 18

3

ere & When: _____ Distance: _____

mments: _____

© Charles Knox/maXximages.com

tip: Myth: Returning runners should run on soft surfaces to prevent injury. Truth: Until stabilizer muscles strengthen, it's better to run on pavement slowly, and walk often.

stance this week: _____ Weight: _____

Distance carried forward:

19 Monday   3!

Where & When: Distance:
Comments:

20 Tuesday   3!

Where & When: Distance:
Comments:

21 Wednesday   3!

Where & When: Distance:
Comments:

22 Thursday   3

Where & When: Distance:
Comments:

23 Friday   3.

Where & When: Distance:
Comments:

December

Saturday 24

59

here & When: _____ Distance: _____

mments: _____

Sunday 25

60

here & When: _____ Distance: _____

mments: _____

tip: So long as you cross the finish line, bring on the bubbly, chocolate, or similar celebratory decadence—even if the race was a personal disaster.

Distance this week: _____ Weight: _____

Distance carried forward:

26 Monday 3

Where & When: Distance:
Comments:

27 Tuesday 3€

Where & When: Distance:
Comments:

28 Wednesday 3€

Where & When: Distance:
Comments:

29 Thursday 36

Where & When: Distance:
Comments:

30 Friday 36

Where & When: Distance:
Comments:

Dec/Jan 2017

Saturday 31

here & When: **Distance:**

mments:

Sunday 1

here & When: **Distance:**

mments:

"In the midst of winter, I found there was within me an invincible summer."

—Albert Camus

tip: Mend the roof before you paint the house. Identify your shortcomings as a runner—name them—and spend some time milling about their priority. Then tackle them one at a time.

otes:

istance this week: **Weight:**

Twelve Months of Running

Jan. 4	Jan. 11	Jan. 18	Jan. 25	Feb. 1	Feb. 8	Feb. 15	Feb. 22	Feb. 29	March 7	March 14	March 21	March 28

To create a cumulative bar graph of weekly mileage,
apply an appropriate scale at the left-hand margin.
Then fill in the bar for each week of running.

Apr. 4	Apr. 11	Apr. 18	Apr. 25	May 2	May 9	May 16	May 23	May 30	June 6	June 13	June 20	June 27

To create a cumulative bar graph of weekly mileage,
apply an appropriate scale at the left-hand margin.
Then fill in the bar for each week of running.

July 4	July 11	July 18	July 25	Aug. 1	Aug. 8	Aug. 15	Aug. 22	Aug. 29	Sept. 5	Sept. 12	Sept. 19	Sept. 26

To create a cumulative bar graph of weekly mileage,
apply an appropriate scale at the left-hand margin.
Then fill in the bar for each week of running.

	Oct. 10	Oct. 17	Oct. 24	Oct. 31	Nov. 7	Nov. 14	Nov. 21	Nov. 28	Dec. 5	Dec. 12	Dec. 19	Dec. 26

A Record of Races

Date	Place	Distance	Time	Pace	Comments & Excuses

A Record of Races

Date	Place	Distance	Time	Pace	Comments & Excuses

RACING

Pace is crucial. And you won't magically find it on race day. If you've resisted using a stopwatch or a heart monitor in your workouts, training for a 10K race is the perfect opportunity to abandon those prejudices.

10K

Warm up? Yes, even a slo half-mile run before the ra is likely to improve your performance, not fatigue you. Remember that a 10k event is too short to gran you a sufficient warm-up during the race.

Divide the race into three equal segments and start slower than you want. Don't reach your race pace until the second segment. Push on the third. But your times between these three segments shouldn't vary by more than 10 percent.

Half Marathon

If you're running a half-marathon as preparation for a marathon, cu your weekly long run to no more than 12 miles and raise the pace.

Every week should include three types of workouts: speed drills, tempo runs, and your long run. Speed drills make you faster. Tempo runs raise your lactate threshold, which will help you maintain a racing pace in the second half of the event. And your weekly long run increases endurance. Toss in some cross training when time allows.

Don't be shaken by early mistakes. If you go out too fast, for example, simply dial back as soon as you recognize your error. It's a long race and there's plenty of time to recover from just about any kind of blunder.

Marathon

No one masters the marathon. Anything can happen on its long tortuous course, which is why it is such a seductive and exciting event. It's in your interest to arrive at the starting line with this humility.

Seek support. Train with a partner or a running group. Get your loved ones to cheer you on at the race. Raise money for a cause. The road to the marathon can be long and lonely. Let others help you get there.

Believe it or not, it's better to undertrain than to overtrain. What you haven't developed by race day can sometimes be overcome with adrenalin and desire. For an overtrained runner, the race is over before it starts.

Get used to crowding. In open water where visibility is often poor, contact with other swimmers is inevitable. On bicycles it can be dangerous. Patience pays. Fighting through a pack of competitors wastes energy and can throw your race into jeopardy. Relax. Your opportunity to pass will come.

Triathlon

Rehearse transitions. Without specific training, it takes bicycling legs longer to reach their running stride than many athletes realize. Pulling dry socks onto wet feet can be an ordeal. Fussing with uncooperative equipment squanders time.

Your weakest event deserves the greatest amount of training effort. Sorry, it's true. Most triathletes use their best event to make up time. The better strategy is not to lose time in your weak event.

JANUARY 2017

_____
_____
_____
_____
_____

FEBRUARY 2017

_____
_____
_____
_____
_____

MARCH 2017

_____
_____
_____
_____
_____

APRIL 2017

_____
_____
_____
_____
_____

MAY 2017

_____
_____
_____
_____
_____

JUNE 2017

_____
_____
_____
_____
_____

JULY 2017

_____
_____
_____
_____
_____

AUGUST 2017

_____
_____
_____
_____
_____

SEPTEMBER 2017

_____
_____
_____
_____
_____

OCTOBER 2017

_____
_____
_____
_____
_____

NOVEMBER 2017

_____
_____
_____
_____
_____

DECEMBER 2017

_____
_____
_____
_____
_____